MANIFESTING MAGICK
WITH
VÉVÉS & SIGILS

CLAUDIA WILLIAMS

LeftHandPress
New Orleans, Louisiana USA

Format Copyright © 2013 Left Hand Press
A subsidiary of Black Moon Publishing, LLC

LeftHandPress.com

Design and layout
by Jo Bounds of Left Hand Press

ISBN: 978-0615822334

United States • United Kingdom • Europe

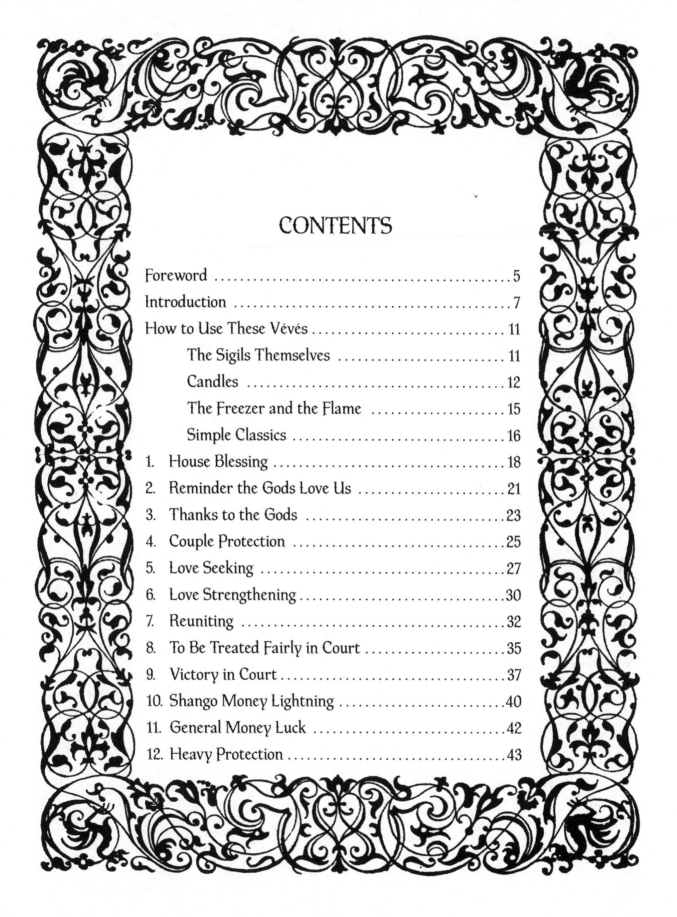

CONTENTS

Foreword 5

Introduction 7

How to Use These Vévés 11

    The Sigils Themselves 11

    Candles 12

    The Freezer and the Flame 15

    Simple Classics 16

1. House Blessing 18

2. Reminder the Gods Love Us 21

3. Thanks to the Gods 23

4. Couple Protection 25

5. Love Seeking 27

6. Love Strengthening 30

7. Reuniting 32

8. To Be Treated Fairly in Court 35

9. Victory in Court 37

10. Shango Money Lightning 40

11. General Money Luck 42

12. Heavy Protection 43

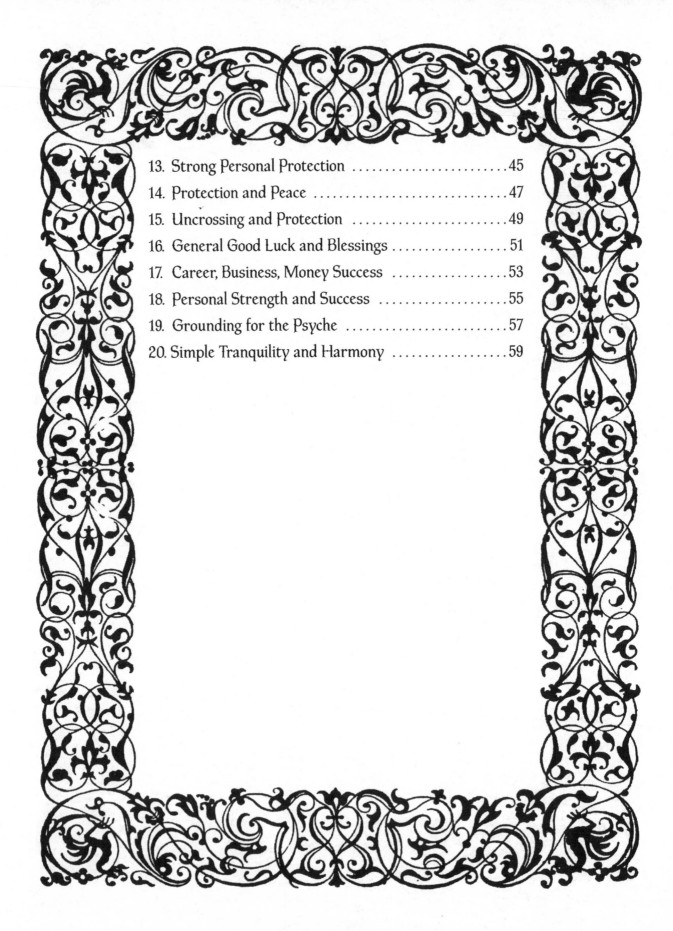

13. Strong Personal Protection 45

14. Protection and Peace 47

15. Uncrossing and Protection 49

16. General Good Luck and Blessings 51

17. Career, Business, Money Success 53

18. Personal Strength and Success 55

19. Grounding for the Psyche 57

20. Simple Tranquility and Harmony 59

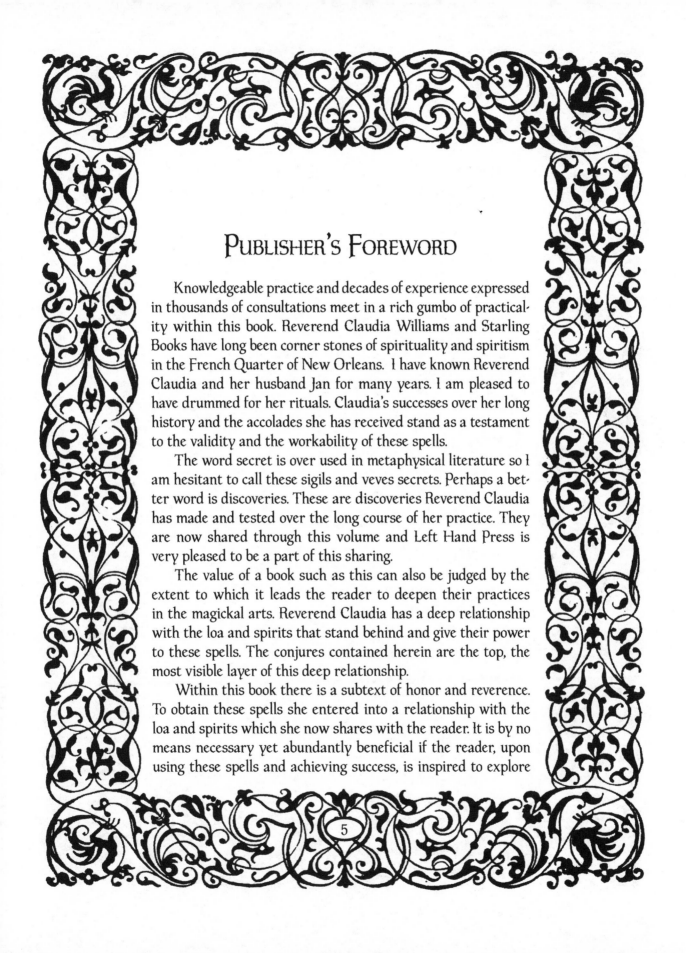

PUBLISHER'S FOREWORD

Knowledgeable practice and decades of experience expressed in thousands of consultations meet in a rich gumbo of practicality within this book. Reverend Claudia Williams and Starling Books have long been corner stones of spirituality and spiritism in the French Quarter of New Orleans. I have known Reverend Claudia and her husband Jan for many years. I am pleased to have drummed for her rituals. Claudia's successes over her long history and the accolades she has received stand as a testament to the validity and the workability of these spells.

The word secret is over used in metaphysical literature so I am hesitant to call these sigils and veves secrets. Perhaps a better word is discoveries. These are discoveries Reverend Claudia has made and tested over the long course of her practice. They are now shared through this volume and Left Hand Press is very pleased to be a part of this sharing.

The value of a book such as this can also be judged by the extent to which it leads the reader to deepen their practices in the magickal arts. Reverend Claudia has a deep relationship with the loa and spirits that stand behind and give their power to these spells. The conjures contained herein are the top, the most visible layer of this deep relationship.

Within this book there is a subtext of honor and reverence. To obtain these spells she entered into a relationship with the loa and spirits which she now shares with the reader. It is by no means necessary yet abundantly beneficial if the reader, upon using these spells and achieving success, is inspired to explore and possibly enter into this kind of deep relationship with the loa or spirits as well. A book such as this can be used as a key to open access to a more complete communication with the Invisibles.

In working their spells one is not alone. Reverend Claudia stands with you in your communion with the spirits and loa.

━━╍╍◆╍╍━━

Left Hand Press is proud to announce that this book is the first in a series of publications to be issued under the heading of "New Orleans Magicks in Theory and Practice." Our aim is to document and offer the reader practitioner access to the living metaphysical practices and traditions as they grow and evolve in the Crescent City.

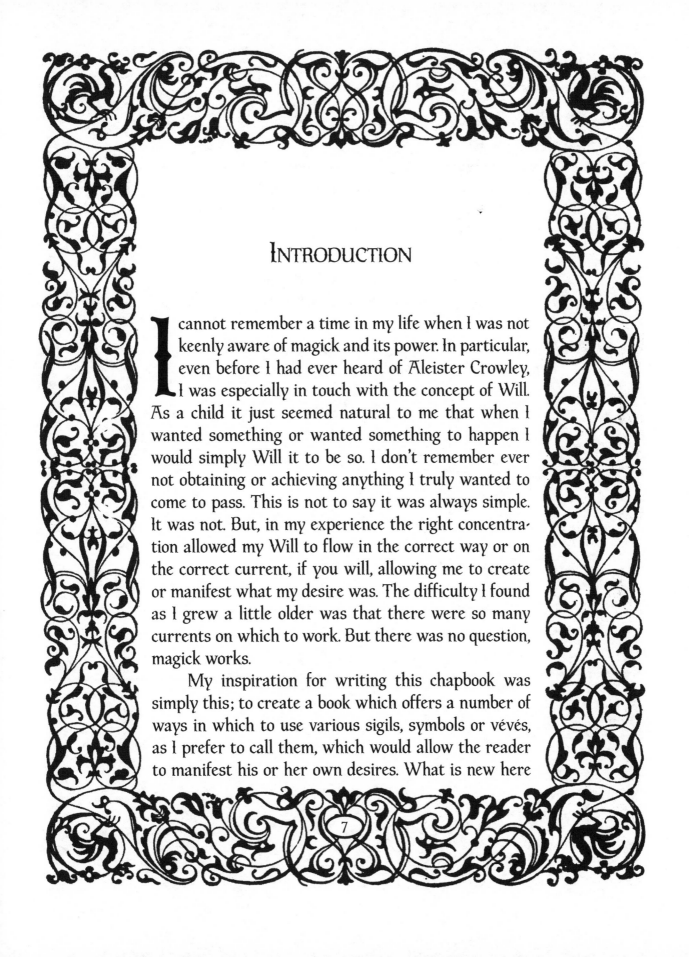

INTRODUCTION

I cannot remember a time in my life when I was not keenly aware of magick and its power. In particular, even before I had ever heard of Aleister Crowley, I was especially in touch with the concept of Will. As a child it just seemed natural to me that when I wanted something or wanted something to happen I would simply Will it to be so. I don't remember ever not obtaining or achieving anything I truly wanted to come to pass. This is not to say it was always simple. It was not. But, in my experience the right concentration allowed my Will to flow in the correct way or on the correct current, if you will, allowing me to create or manifest what my desire was. The difficulty I found as I grew a little older was that there were so many currents on which to work. But there was no question, magick works.

My inspiration for writing this chapbook was simply this; to create a book which offers a number of ways in which to use various sigils, symbols or vévés, as I prefer to call them, which would allow the reader to manifest his or her own desires. What is new here

is that the reader may not be familiar with some of the ways to use these symbols and they definitely will not know these vévés, because they are all my own designs. They were created over the years inspired by my own needs and the needs of my clients. The sigils contained here have proven themselves time and again.

The more difficult problem became describing the premise on which these designs work to the reader. Are they Vodou, Santeria (my own areas of practice), Witchcraft, Thelemic, New Age (Gods forbid) or any number of other possible practices and traditions? The truth is, they contain elements of all of these systems. When I designed them over the years there was an important reason for this. They had to be symbols which people could identify with on many levels, from many perspectives. They had to be universally accessible. I believe this has been accomplished and that it actually makes the magick they help manifest stronger because of it. Therefore, as you look through this chapbook you will note various influences in each of the symbols. No doubt you will be familiar with at least a few even if you consider yourself a magickal novice. Some will not be familiar, but each one is fully explained so that you may come to understand it. Understanding the symbols, items, etc. used in any form of magickal working is, I have found, essential for the work to be successful. People must not only use things, but understand why they are using them for the work to really connect

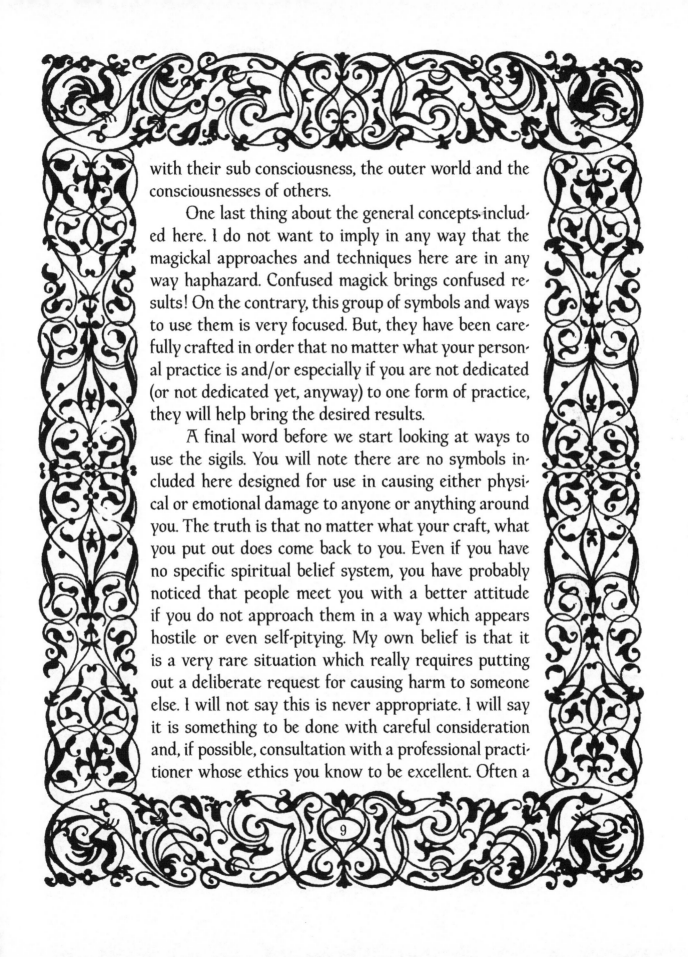

with their sub consciousness, the outer world and the consciousnesses of others.

One last thing about the general concepts included here. I do not want to imply in any way that the magickal approaches and techniques here are in any way haphazard. Confused magick brings confused results! On the contrary, this group of symbols and ways to use them is very focused. But, they have been carefully crafted in order that no matter what your personal practice is and/or especially if you are not dedicated (or not dedicated yet, anyway) to one form of practice, they will help bring the desired results.

A final word before we start looking at ways to use the sigils. You will note there are no symbols included here designed for use in causing either physical or emotional damage to anyone or anything around you. The truth is that no matter what your craft, what you put out does come back to you. Even if you have no specific spiritual belief system, you have probably noticed that people meet you with a better attitude if you do not approach them in a way which appears hostile or even self-pitying. My own belief is that it is a very rare situation which really requires putting out a deliberate request for causing harm to someone else. I will not say this is never appropriate. I will say it is something to be done with careful consideration and, if possible, consultation with a professional practitioner whose ethics you know to be excellent. Often a situation which might appear to need this sort of work can actually be remedied in a way much safer for all involved. This is not meant to be a lesson in ethics and values, it is a matter of practicality.

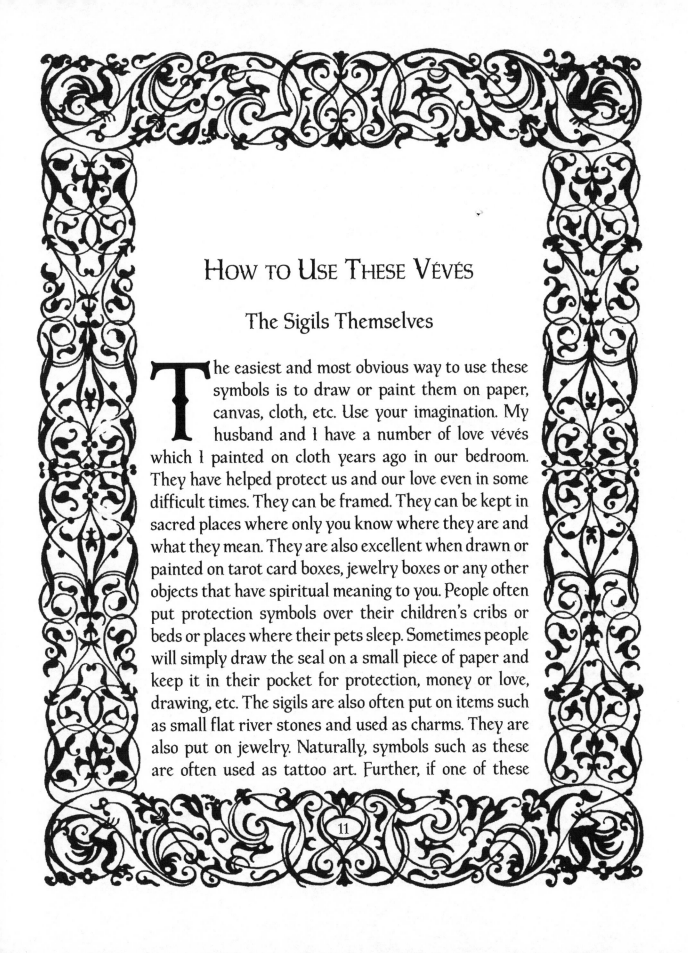

How to Use These Vévés

The Sigils Themselves

The easiest and most obvious way to use these symbols is to draw or paint them on paper, canvas, cloth, etc. Use your imagination. My husband and I have a number of love vévés which I painted on cloth years ago in our bedroom. They have helped protect us and our love even in some difficult times. They can be framed. They can be kept in sacred places where only you know where they are and what they mean. They are also excellent when drawn or painted on tarot card boxes, jewelry boxes or any other objects that have spiritual meaning to you. People often put protection symbols over their children's cribs or beds or places where their pets sleep. Sometimes people will simply draw the seal on a small piece of paper and keep it in their pocket for protection, money or love, drawing, etc. The sigils are also often put on items such as small flat river stones and used as charms. They are also put on jewelry. Naturally, symbols such as these are often used as tattoo art. Further, if one of these

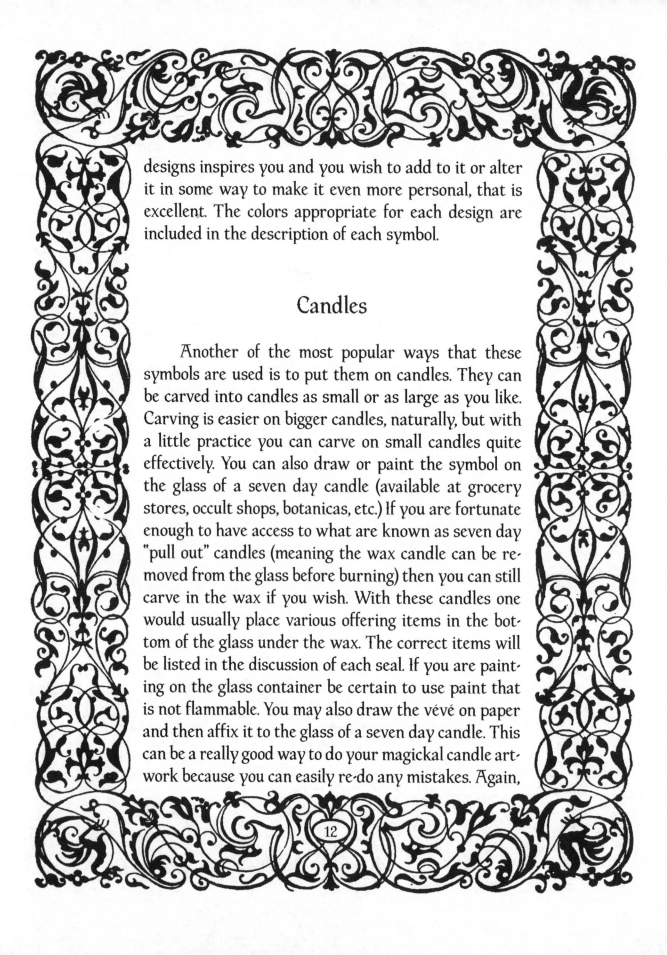

designs inspires you and you wish to add to it or alter it in some way to make it even more personal, that is excellent. The colors appropriate for each design are included in the description of each symbol.

Candles

Another of the most popular ways that these symbols are used is to put them on candles. They can be carved into candles as small or as large as you like. Carving is easier on bigger candles, naturally, but with a little practice you can carve on small candles quite effectively. You can also draw or paint the symbol on the glass of a seven day candle (available at grocery stores, occult shops, botanicas, etc.) If you are fortunate enough to have access to what are known as seven day "pull out" candles (meaning the wax candle can be removed from the glass before burning) then you can still carve in the wax if you wish. With these candles one would usually place various offering items in the bottom of the glass under the wax. The correct items will be listed in the discussion of each seal. If you are painting on the glass container be certain to use paint that is not flammable. You may also draw the vévé on paper and then affix it to the glass of a seven day candle. This can be a really good way to do your magickal candle artwork because you can easily re-do any mistakes. Again,

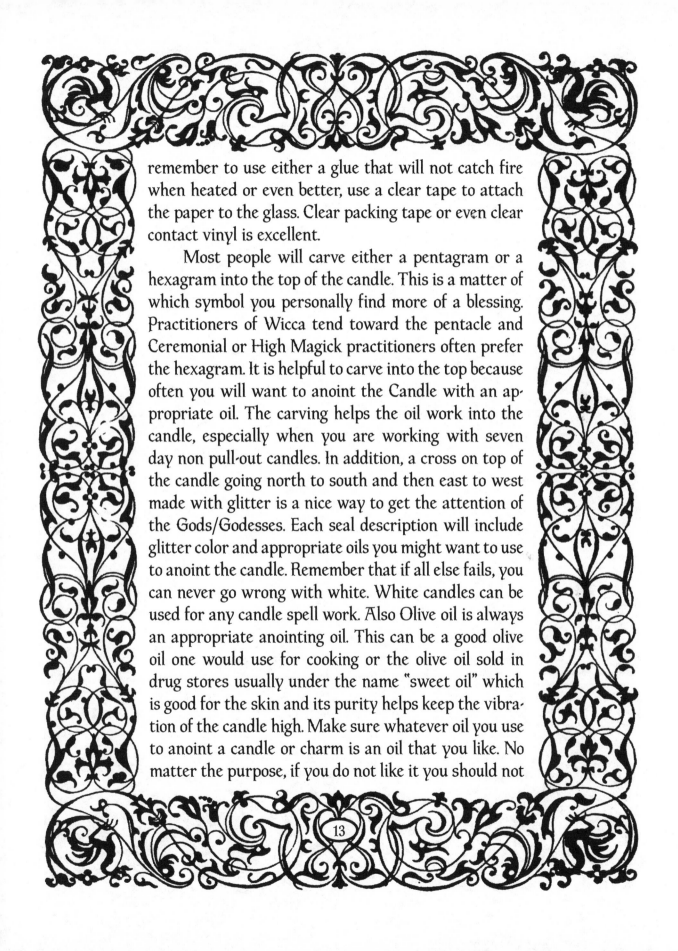

remember to use either a glue that will not catch fire when heated or even better, use a clear tape to attach the paper to the glass. Clear packing tape or even clear contact vinyl is excellent.

Most people will carve either a pentagram or a hexagram into the top of the candle. This is a matter of which symbol you personally find more of a blessing. Practitioners of Wicca tend toward the pentacle and Ceremonial or High Magick practitioners often prefer the hexagram. It is helpful to carve into the top because often you will want to anoint the Candle with an appropriate oil. The carving helps the oil work into the candle, especially when you are working with seven day non pull-out candles. In addition, a cross on top of the candle going north to south and then east to west made with glitter is a nice way to get the attention of the Gods/Godesses. Each seal description will include glitter color and appropriate oils you might want to use to anoint the candle. Remember that if all else fails, you can never go wrong with white. White candles can be used for any candle spell work. Also Olive oil is always an appropriate anointing oil. This can be a good olive oil one would use for cooking or the olive oil sold in drug stores usually under the name "sweet oil" which is good for the skin and its purity helps keep the vibration of the candle high. Make sure whatever oil you use to anoint a candle or charm is an oil that you like. No matter the purpose, if you do not like it you should not

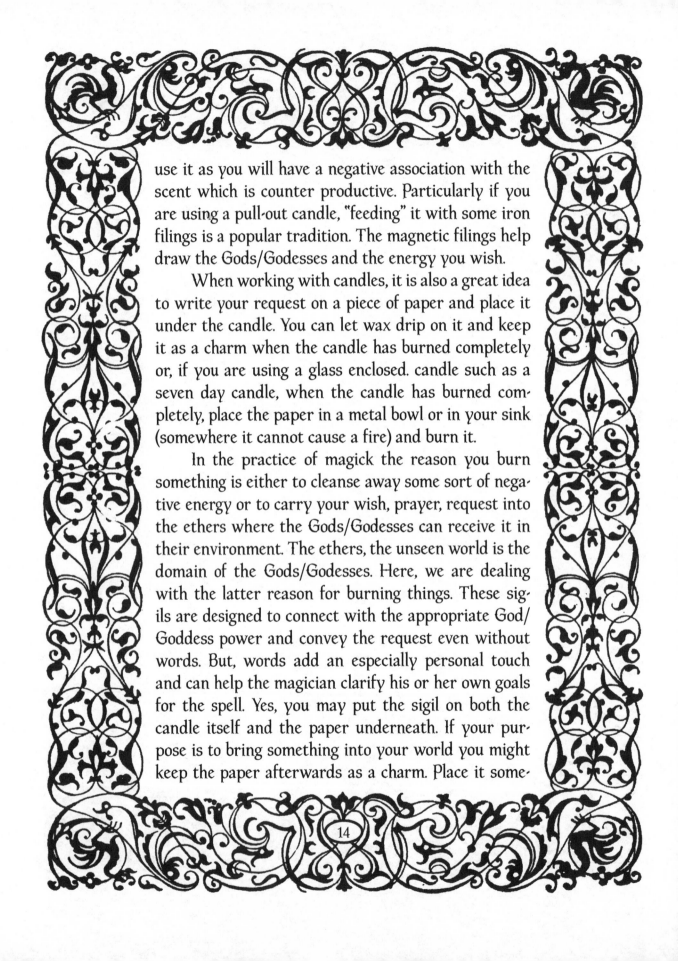

use it as you will have a negative association with the scent which is counter productive. Particularly if you are using a pull-out candle, "feeding" it with some iron filings is a popular tradition. The magnetic filings help draw the Gods/Godesses and the energy you wish.

When working with candles, it is also a great idea to write your request on a piece of paper and place it under the candle. You can let wax drip on it and keep it as a charm when the candle has burned completely or, if you are using a glass enclosed. candle such as a seven day candle, when the candle has burned completely, place the paper in a metal bowl or in your sink (somewhere it cannot cause a fire) and burn it.

In the practice of magick the reason you burn something is either to cleanse away some sort of negative energy or to carry your wish, prayer, request into the ethers where the Gods/Godesses can receive it in their environment. The ethers, the unseen world is the domain of the Gods/Godesses. Here, we are dealing with the latter reason for burning things. These sigils are designed to connect with the appropriate God/Goddess power and convey the request even without words. But, words add an especially personal touch and can help the magician clarify his or her own goals for the spell. Yes, you may put the sigil on both the candle itself and the paper underneath. If your purpose is to bring something into your world you might keep the paper afterwards as a charm. Place it somewhere it will not be disturbed. If you are working to remove something from your life, burning the paper at the end of the spell is often a really nice way of bringing a very physical closure to the situation. These are simple visualization techniques that most people find have a strong effect on them. It can be very gratifying to watch something you want to rid yourself of go up in flame, even if it is on a symbolic level.

The Freezer and The Flame

We have already considered the use of fire in association with sigil magick. To carry a wish to the Gods/Godesses, to rid yourself of an issue, irritation, bad habit, etc. fire can be most useful and even inspiring. But, one of the greatest and most under appreciated magickal devices around is the refrigerator, or even better, the freezer. If you want to put an end to a problem, bad habit, bad influence, draw the appropriate symbol for your purpose on a piece of paper. If you wish, add a photograph, write a request for how you want this issue to become a non-issue. It is usually best to put everything in a small zip lock freezer bag. (Some of my clients have some of the most interesting items in their freezers). Knowing that you have put something on permanent "hold" is a nice feeling. This is also an excellent thing to do when you aren't sure what you want. For example, a reconciliation symbol drawn in a

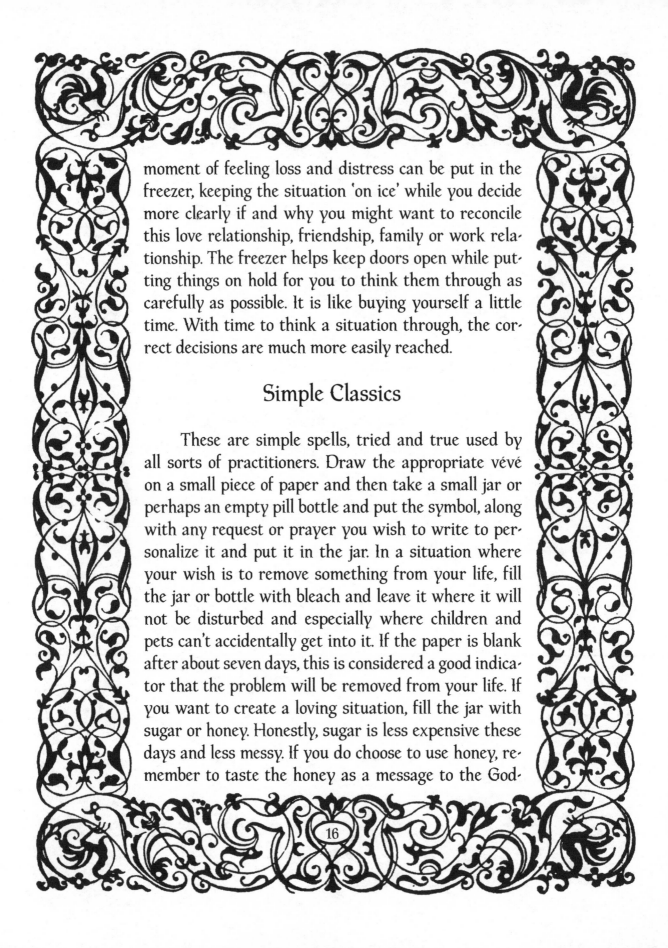

moment of feeling loss and distress can be put in the freezer, keeping the situation 'on ice' while you decide more clearly if and why you might want to reconcile this love relationship, friendship, family or work relationship. The freezer helps keep doors open while putting things on hold for you to think them through as carefully as possible. It is like buying yourself a little time. With time to think a situation through, the correct decisions are much more easily reached.

Simple Classics

These are simple spells, tried and true used by all sorts of practitioners. Draw the appropriate vévé on a small piece of paper and then take a small jar or perhaps an empty pill bottle and put the symbol, along with any request or prayer you wish to write to personalize it and put it in the jar. In a situation where your wish is to remove something from your life, fill the jar or bottle with bleach and leave it where it will not be disturbed and especially where children and pets can't accidentally get into it. If the paper is blank after about seven days, this is considered a good indicator that the problem will be removed from your life. If you want to create a loving situation, fill the jar with sugar or honey. Honestly, sugar is less expensive these days and less messy. If you do choose to use honey, remember to taste the honey as a message to the Goddess/Orisha Osun that the honey is untainted. Osun works with love issues, but once had an attempt made on her life by someone giving her her favorite food, honey and poisoning it. In honor to her, you always taste the honey before you give it to her or any other Gods (they all know the story). If it is a matter of protection, fill the jar with salt. Sea salt or black salt are even better if you can get them. Or, a mixture of salts is fine. In any case, tradition dictates that you give a spell up to nine weeks to work. After nine weeks of the pill bottle or jar having been left alone you may discard the whole jar. DO NOT reuse the bleach, sugar, honey or salts. You may, if you wish, put some of the protection salt in a sachet or gris-gris bag for protection for the same person you did the spell to protect. You may do the same sort of thing with sugar. Honey and bleach should be properly discarded.

Now you have some really good traditional ways to use the symbols. Certainly, you will come up with additional methods which are very personal and powerful to you alone. In fact, I encourage you to do so. Now, on to the sigils themselves.

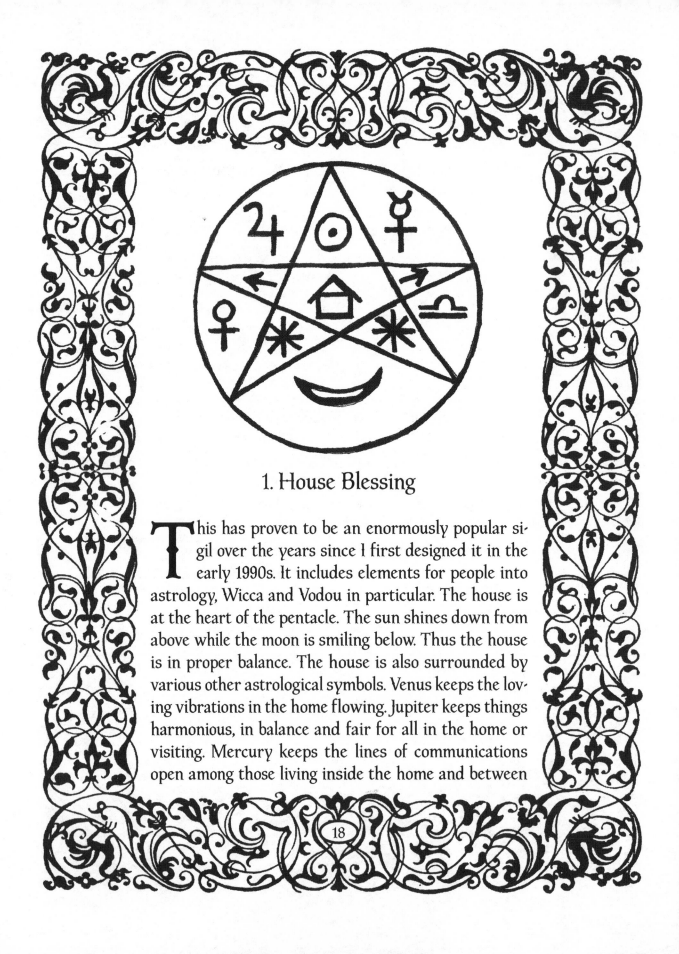

1. House Blessing

This has proven to be an enormously popular sigil over the years since I first designed it in the
early 1990s. It includes elements for people into
astrology, Wicca and Vodou in particular. The house is
at the heart of the pentacle. The sun shines down from
above while the moon is smiling below. Thus the house
is in proper balance. The house is also surrounded by
various other astrological symbols. Venus keeps the loving vibrations in the home flowing. Jupiter keeps things
harmonious, in balance and fair for all in the home or
visiting. Mercury keeps the lines of communications
open among those living inside the home and between

those inside and the outside world. The symbol for Libra also helps maintain a sense of balance. The house then radiates its joy and loving vibrations out to the rest of the world. This helps those who live inside the house to carry their positive energy out into the world to help benefit others. The star or asterisk-like symbols are life symbols affirming positive energy on all levels inside and outside the home. The colors to be used with this sign are yellow and blue. If you want to bring more joy to your home an emphasis on yellow is what you want. If you want to calm things down, after there have been arguments, visits from negative people, difficult relatives, etc. then blue is the color to emphasize. The glitter color to top this candle with is gold. However, if there have been strong angry feelings between people living in the home or from visitors, silver can be very calming. We have our own blends of oils including one called House Blessing oil which can be used to anoint candles or items on which you might use this symbol. Here in New Orleans oils such as Marie Laveau Voodoo luck oil and Van Van oil (also a popular Vodou blessing oil) are used frequently in association with house blessing. Tonka Bean, Jasmine, Lavender, Frankincense or Myrrh oils would also be appropriate. And yes, you can use a mixture of Frankincense and Myrrh. This sigil may also be used for help in buying or selling a house. If you are hoping to buy a new home list the qualities and features you are looking for and

use orange and brown (a color of houses, grounding, home base.) You might also want to add a sigil like the one for Career/Financial Success with deep green if you are trying to get a loan, mortgage, etc. If you want to sell your home you might use the House Blessing seal and one of the money seals such as the Shango Money Lightning or General Money luck with deep green, yellow and gold. Add your own spell words or prayer for selling your home.

2. Reminder the Gods/Goddesses Love Us

This is a sigil very good for people when they get "the blues." A great way to lift the spirits of a friend or loved one is to give them a gift with this design on it. This one is quite simple. Two stars and the astrological sign for the sun shine onto the person who is feeling unloved. We are all angels with big hearts; whether you are into angels on a spiritual level or not, the concept is easy to appreciate. Personally, I must admit that I am not really an "angel" person. The connotation angels have had since the 1980s and the

connection to the standard New Age concepts have left me rather bored. I find the whole "angel" movement a little too sugary sweet for my own sensibilities. However, when I have clients whose moods are very low, I have found there is a strong power in calling them "angels" and reminding them they are all part of the Gods/Godesses and the They do not wish them to suffer. So, the potency of this design has been known to surprise people (even me!) White is an excellent color here. The glitter colors you might use on top of a candle are gold or one of the new iridescent white or silver/blue glitters so popular now. This is one for which honey or sugar is certainly an appropriate "food." A lodestone for good luck, clear quartz for cleansing bad feelings, rose quartz for a loving attitude or amethyst for self love and heart healing are all appropriate to add if you like. The anointing oils would be Frankincense, Myrrh (separately or together), Allspice (a great spirit lifter). Sage or Rosemary, for giving a sense of strength through difficulty would also be fine. Our own Nine Fruits of Life at Starling would also be a good anointing choice.

3. Thanks to the Gods/Goddesses

Sometimes we just feel blessed; the Gods/Godesses have answered a prayer or request we have put out and we want to express our gratitude. This symbol is for doing just that. It works very nicely to draw this and burn a white candle behind it. Basically, the message here is that your cup runneth over and you appreciate it. The design includes the pentacle, a cross, which you can draw square as I have, (this would be used in Vodou and Native American spiritualities) or with an elongated base like a Christian cross. The star symbols are symbols of life in many traditions. Colors to use when drawing or if you are making a candle

would be yellow, gold, light green, pink if you're feeling very loving. Gold glitter for the top of this one. If you wish to anoint a candle or the paper design, use an oil that you love. You are telling the Gods/Godesses thank you and so you want to share things you love and are grateful for with them. The same would be true here for any feeding of a candle you might do. If you love it, share a little with your Gods/Godesses, they will appreciate the thought.

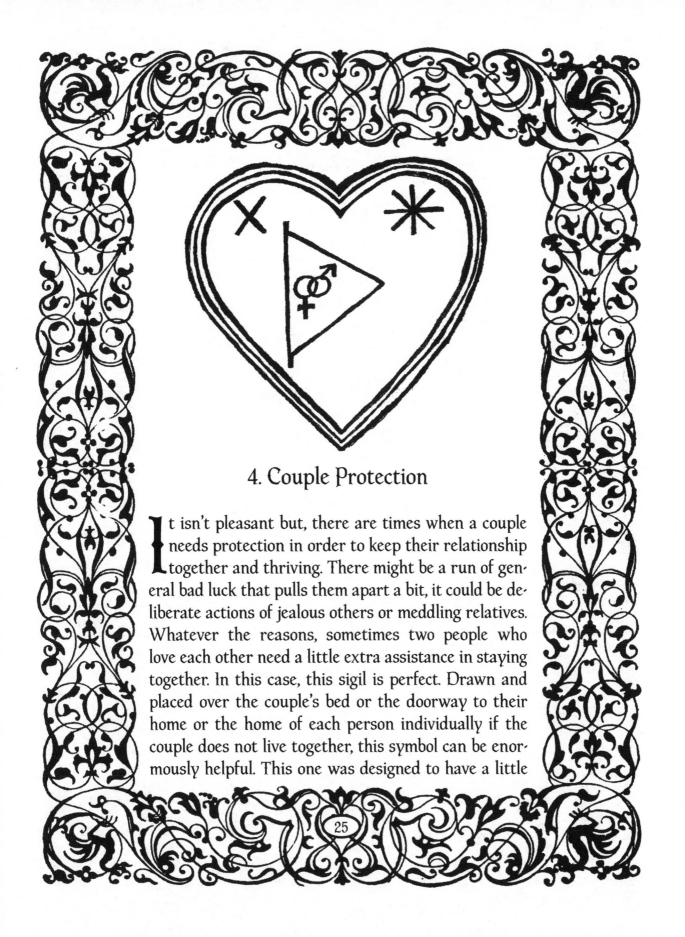

4. Couple Protection

It isn't pleasant but, there are times when a couple needs protection in order to keep their relationship together and thriving. There might be a run of general bad luck that pulls them apart a bit, it could be deliberate actions of jealous others or meddling relatives. Whatever the reasons, sometimes two people who love each other need a little extra assistance in staying together. In this case, this sigil is perfect. Drawn and placed over the couple's bed or the doorway to their home or the home of each person individually if the couple does not live together, this symbol can be enormously helpful. This one was designed to have a little something for everyone. The symbols for male and female or Venus and Mars are linked representing the couple. In the case of a gay or lesbian couple simply use two linked Venus or Mars symbols instead. The couple is housed inside Thurisaz, the "gateway" rune also known for its strength. This represents the couple embarking on their battle to stay united against various forces trying to trouble them. Above and to the left is Gebo, the rune of partnership and gift (think of a blessed partnership). To the right of the Thurisaz rune is a Voudon symbol of life and blessings. These are all contained in a three ringed heart. The couple are inside each other's hearts and protected by the three rings so that whatever negativity is directed toward them is sent back to its originator three fold. Colors for this vévé are white and/or black for the protective elements. The background can be pink or yellow. Red, with some of the other colors, is appropriate if the couple is really angry at what they feel is being sent to them. The three rings of the heart can be gold, black, red, yellow or gold and silver together. Gold is the glitter color for the top of a candle. Protection, Venus, Myrrh, Vetiver or Sandalwood would all be appropriate anointing oils. Honey is a great offering if you are feeding a candle. Five pennies are also appropriate as Osun, the love Goddess Orisha loves gold and copper and her number is five.

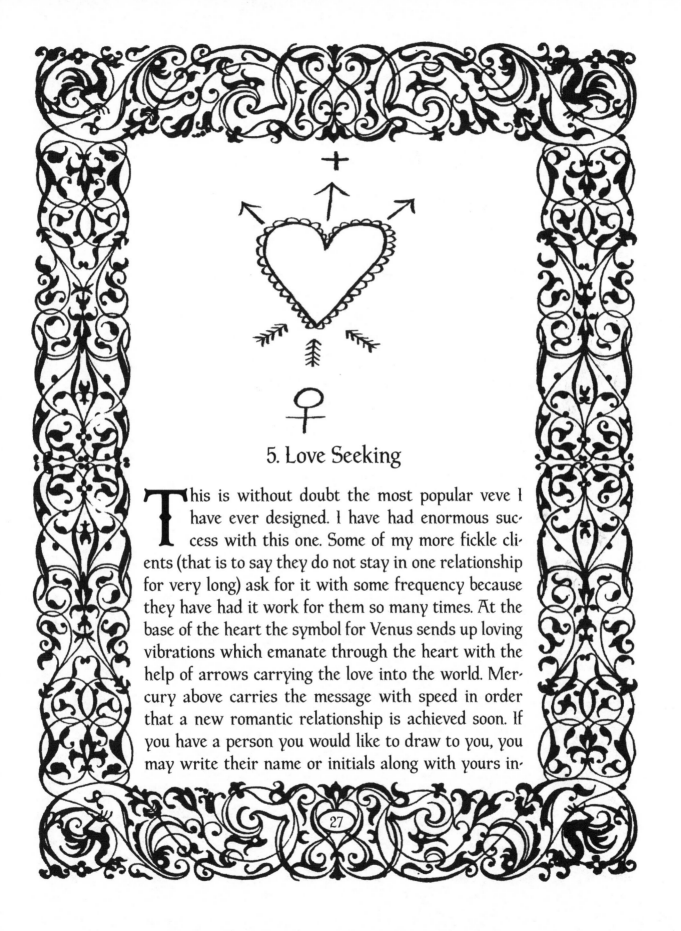

5. Love Seeking

This is without doubt the most popular veve I have ever designed. I have had enormous success with this one. Some of my more fickle clients (that is to say they do not stay in one relationship for very long) ask for it with some frequency because they have had it work for them so many times. At the base of the heart the symbol for Venus sends up loving vibrations which emanate through the heart with the help of arrows carrying the love into the world. Mercury above carries the message with speed in order that a new romantic relationship is achieved soon. If you have a person you would like to draw to you, you may write their name or initials along with yours inside the heart. If you have no one special in mind, leave that area blank. Either way, often this sigil will bring a few people for you to choose from (the Gods/Godesses like us to have choices.) Please remember to be thoughtful and not play with other people's emotions. If you want something more sexual and less long-term relationship oriented, red is the color to use. Remember to be clear with the person that this is what you are interested in. If you are looking for a more sturdy relationship, use pink. If you are not sure exactly what you want, use orange or white. Venus and Mercury both share green as their colors although Venus loves pinks and reds and yellows also. A little black or navy for mystery and a little protection of the heart is fine. The color for the candle top glitter would be gold and, if you like, red as well. The best oil to use with this design is by far a good traditional Come To Me, Desire Me, Venus, Satyr/Pan, Attraction, Cinnamon, Rose or Jasmine would all be good anointing oil choices as well. If you wish to leave offerings with this sigil or feed a candle, lodestone for attraction is excellent. Again, this is Osun's territory so honey and five pennies would be very pleasing to her. She also loves flowers, especially yellow ones. This is also a vévé very much suited to Haitian Vodou Goddess/Lwa, Erzulie. She probably originated out of Osun. At any rate you might also offer some champagne (pink is a favorite), cookies, cake or candy and a bottle of perfume.

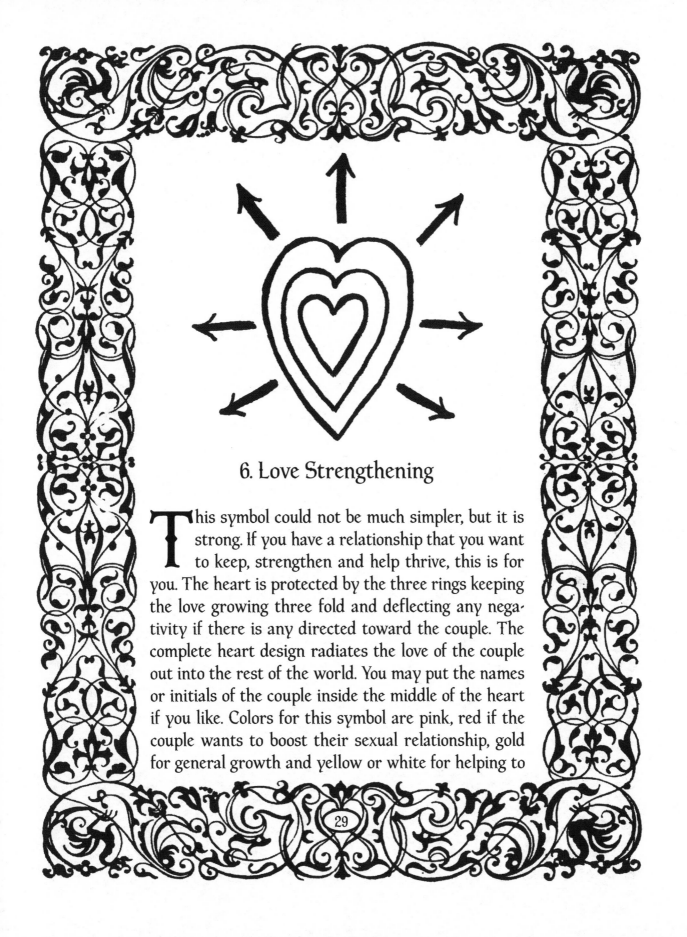

6. Love Strengthening

This symbol could not be much simpler, but it is strong. If you have a relationship that you want to keep, strengthen and help thrive, this is for you. The heart is protected by the three rings keeping the love growing three fold and deflecting any negativity if there is any directed toward the couple. The complete heart design radiates the love of the couple out into the rest of the world. You may put the names or initials of the couple inside the middle of the heart if you like. Colors for this symbol are pink, red if the couple wants to boost their sexual relationship, gold for general growth and yellow or white for helping to mend feelings after an argument. Gold glitter on the top of a candle. Venus , Isis, Cinnamon, Amber, Orange, Myrrh or Sandalwood oil would all be good anointing choices. The same offerings to feed a candle that are appropriate for the Love Seeking vévé are also appropriate here.

7. Reuniting

This symbol is best used for mending and reuniting friendships, family relationships, problems with co-workers. It can be used to mend romantic relationships, but for that I would recommend using the Love Strengthening or Couple Protection sigils. This can be a useful seal if you have lost a pet or even (Gods forbid), a child. Since the vast majority of children who are kidnapped in the United States are taken by a noncustodial parent, this sigil can be helpful on several levels. It can help reunite the child with the parent who is supposed to have custody while also opening better doors of communication between the parents which

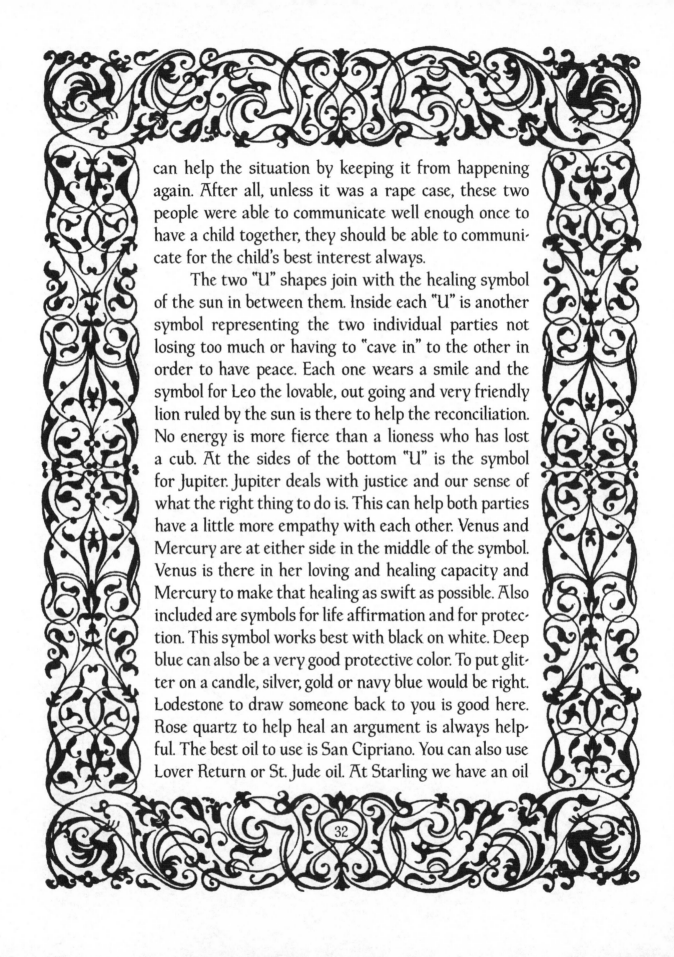

can help the situation by keeping it from happening
again. After all, unless it was a rape case, these two
people were able to communicate well enough once to
have a child together, they should be able to communicate for the child's best interest always.

The two "U" shapes join with the healing symbol
of the sun in between them. Inside each "U" is another
symbol representing the two individual parties not
losing too much or having to "cave in" to the other in
order to have peace. Each one wears a smile and the
symbol for Leo the lovable, out going and very friendly
lion ruled by the sun is there to help the reconciliation.
No energy is more fierce than a lioness who has lost
a cub. At the sides of the bottom "U" is the symbol
for Jupiter. Jupiter deals with justice and our sense of
what the right thing to do is. This can help both parties
have a little more empathy with each other. Venus and
Mercury are at either side in the middle of the symbol.
Venus is there in her loving and healing capacity and
Mercury to make that healing as swift as possible. Also
included are symbols for life affirmation and for protection. This symbol works best with black on white. Deep
blue can also be a very good protective color. To put glitter on a candle, silver, gold or navy blue would be right.
Lodestone to draw someone back to you is good here.
Rose quartz to help heal an argument is always helpful. The best oil to use is San Cipriano. You can also use
Lover Return or St. Jude oil. At Starling we have an oil

called Impossible Dream for difficult situations which works really well, Healing, Venus, Lodestone, Frankincense and Myrrh together, or Allspice oil would each be good choices too. Remember to approach this situation with as much of an open heart as possible and ready to make at least a little bit of a compromise.

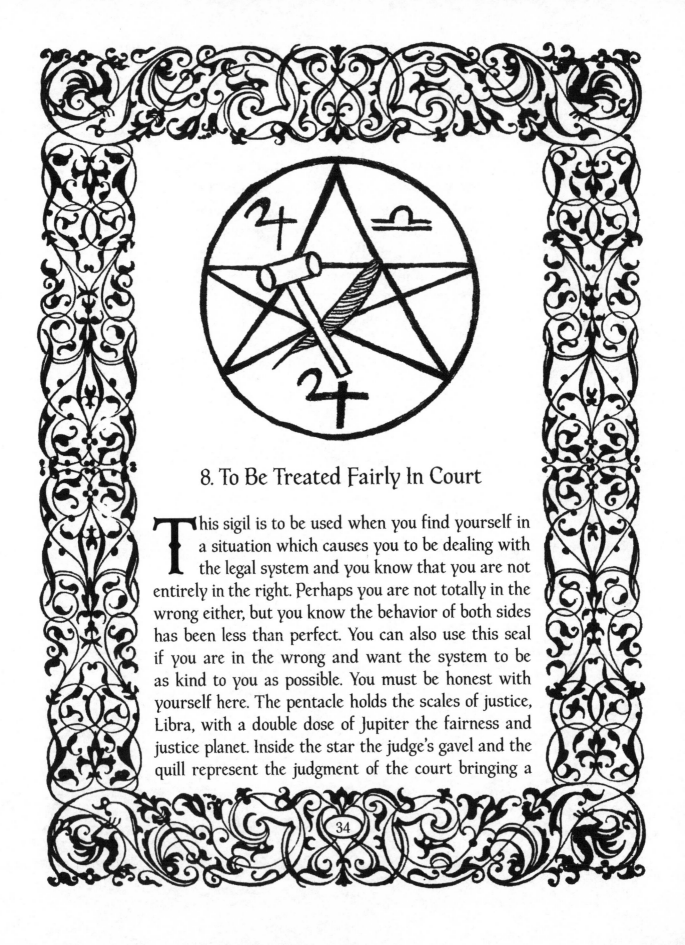

8. To Be Treated Fairly In Court

This sigil is to be used when you find yourself in a situation which causes you to be dealing with the legal system and you know that you are not entirely in the right. Perhaps you are not totally in the wrong either, but you know the behavior of both sides has been less than perfect. You can also use this seal if you are in the wrong and want the system to be as kind to you as possible. You must be honest with yourself here. The pentacle holds the scales of justice, Libra, with a double dose of Jupiter the fairness and justice planet. Inside the star the judge's gavel and the quill represent the judgment of the court bringing a

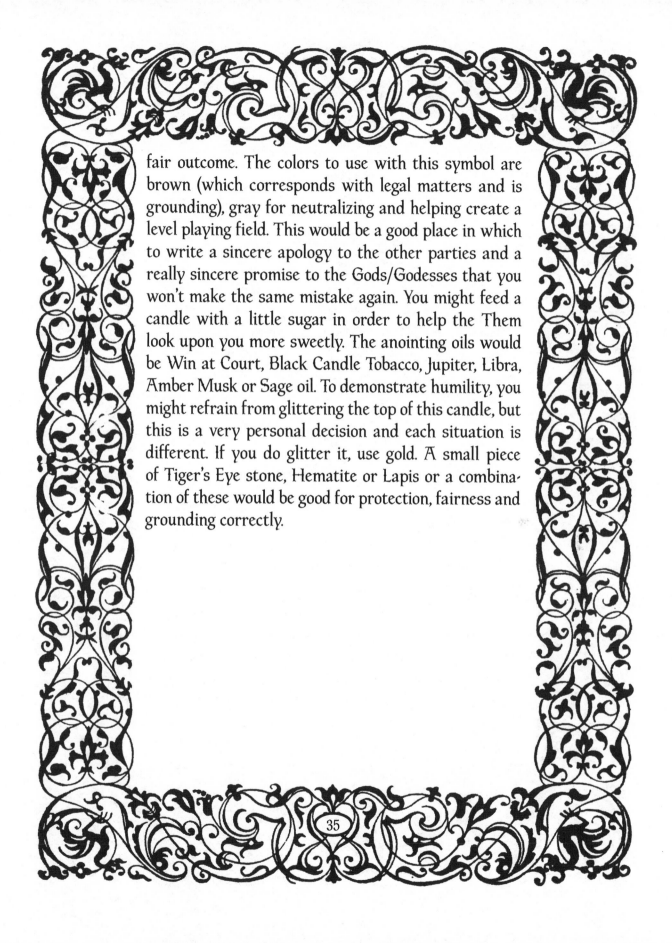

fair outcome. The colors to use with this symbol are brown (which corresponds with legal matters and is grounding), gray for neutralizing and helping create a level playing field. This would be a good place in which to write a sincere apology to the other parties and a really sincere promise to the Gods/Godesses that you won't make the same mistake again. You might feed a candle with a little sugar in order to help the Them look upon you more sweetly. The anointing oils would be Win at Court, Black Candle Tobacco, Jupiter, Libra, Amber Musk or Sage oil. To demonstrate humility, you might refrain from glittering the top of this candle, but this is a very personal decision and each situation is different. If you do glitter it, use gold. A small piece of Tiger's Eye stone, Hematite or Lapis or a combination of these would be good for protection, fairness and grounding correctly.

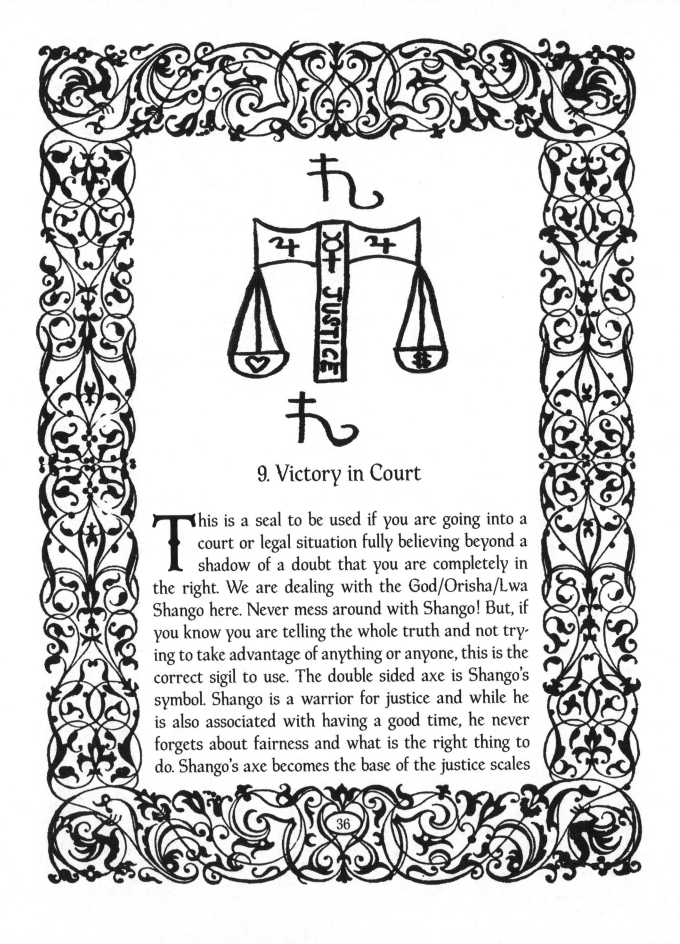

9. Victory in Court

This is a seal to be used if you are going into a court or legal situation fully believing beyond a shadow of a doubt that you are completely in the right. We are dealing with the God/Orisha/Lwa Shango here. Never mess around with Shango! But, if you know you are telling the whole truth and not trying to take advantage of anything or anyone, this is the correct sigil to use. The double sided axe is Shango's symbol. Shango is a warrior for justice and while he is also associated with having a good time, he never forgets about fairness and what is the right thing to do. Shango's axe becomes the base of the justice scales

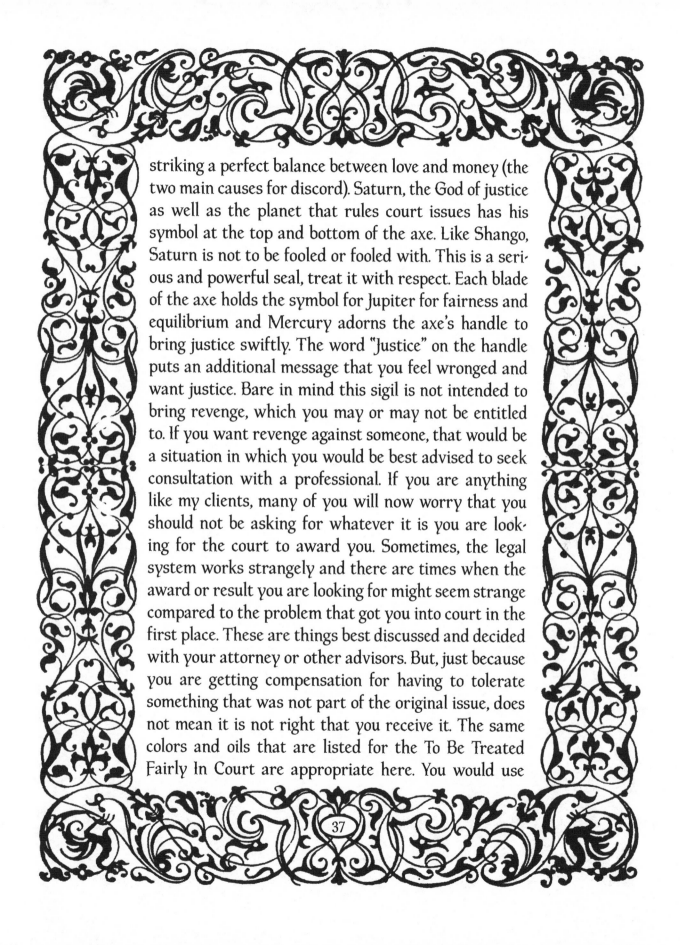

striking a perfect balance between love and money (the two main causes for discord). Saturn, the God of justice as well as the planet that rules court issues has his symbol at the top and bottom of the axe. Like Shango, Saturn is not to be fooled or fooled with. This is a serious and powerful seal, treat it with respect. Each blade of the axe holds the symbol for Jupiter for fairness and equilibrium and Mercury adorns the axe's handle to bring justice swiftly. The word "Justice" on the handle puts an additional message that you feel wronged and want justice. Bare in mind this sigil is not intended to bring revenge, which you may or may not be entitled to. If you want revenge against someone, that would be a situation in which you would be best advised to seek consultation with a professional. If you are anything like my clients, many of you will now worry that you should not be asking for whatever it is you are looking for the court to award you. Sometimes, the legal system works strangely and there are times when the award or result you are looking for might seem strange compared to the problem that got you into court in the first place. These are things best discussed and decided with your attorney or other advisors. But, just because you are getting compensation for having to tolerate something that was not part of the original issue, does not mean it is not right that you receive it. The same colors and oils that are listed for the To Be Treated Fairly In Court are appropriate here. You would use

gold glitter to top the candle. The same stones are correct as well. If you want to release some extra anger, draw the sigil in red, white, silver or gold on red paper. (White and red are two of Shango's colors).

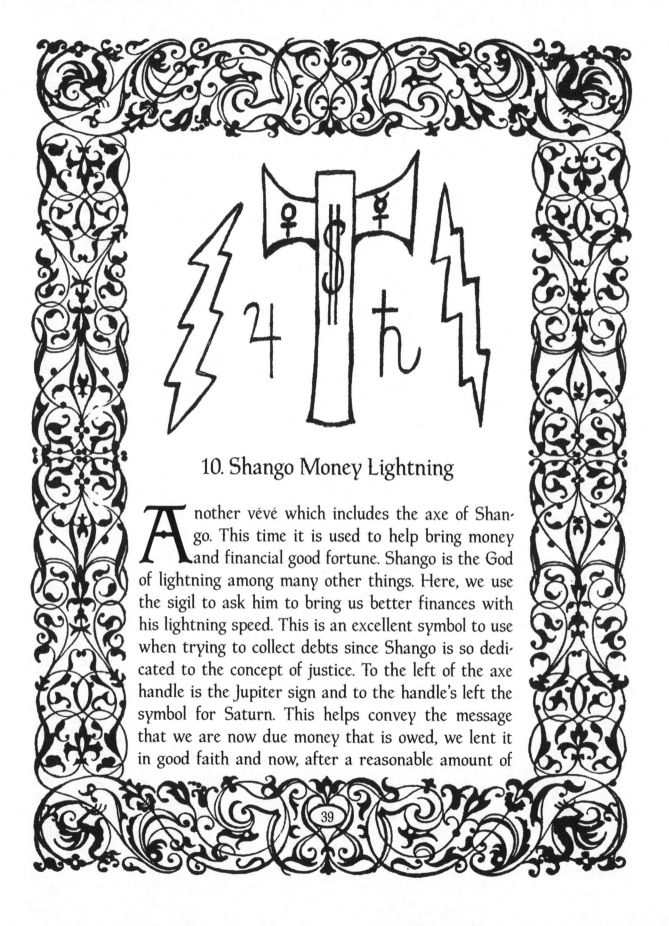

10. Shango Money Lightning

Another vévé which includes the axe of Shango. This time it is used to help bring money and financial good fortune. Shango is the God of lightning among many other things. Here, we use the sigil to ask him to bring us better finances with his lightning speed. This is an excellent symbol to use when trying to collect debts since Shango is so dedicated to the concept of justice. To the left of the axe handle is the Jupiter sign and to the handle's left the symbol for Saturn. This helps convey the message that we are now due money that is owed, we lent it in good faith and now, after a reasonable amount of time to allow the borrower to accumulate the funds, it's time for us to be paid back. Venus on the left blade is a money Goddess and Mercury on the right blade is able to bring the money back swiftly adding to the lightning quickness and force that is Shango's. The dollar symbol in the middle is one that virtually everyone recognizes and understands. Colors to use for drawing or candle carving are green, red (which is not only one of Shango's colors, but also the Asian color for wealth) gold (as in coins), and orange for attracting/drawing. Top a candle with gold, red or green glitter. The oils for anointing would be Money Drawing, Shango, Attraction, Pine, Patchouli or Cinnamon oil.

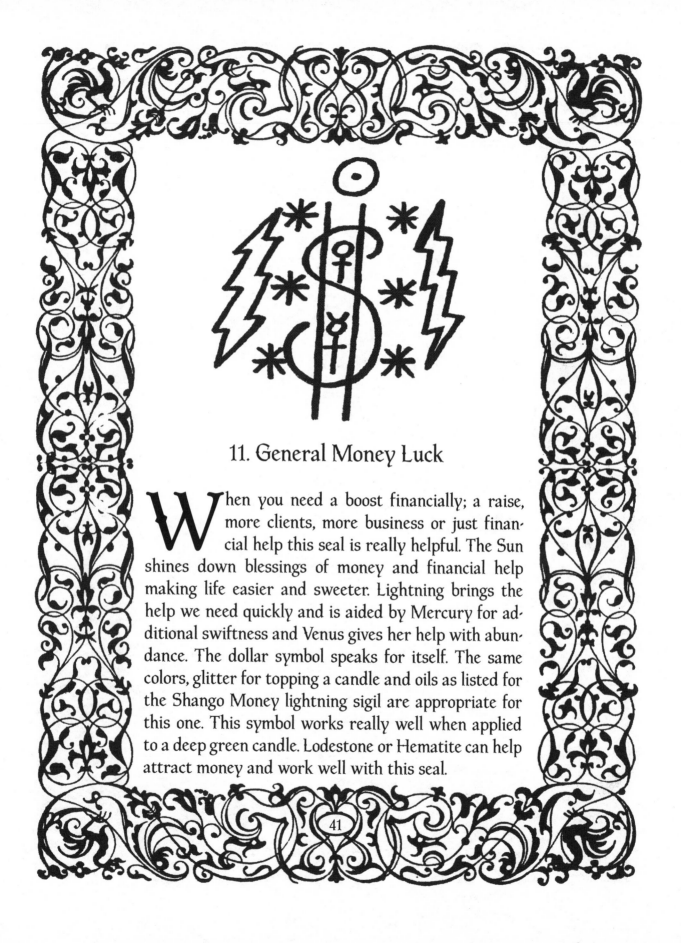

11. General Money Luck

When you need a boost financially; a raise, more clients, more business or just financial help this seal is really helpful. The Sun shines down blessings of money and financial help making life easier and sweeter. Lightning brings the help we need quickly and is aided by Mercury for additional swiftness and Venus gives her help with abundance. The dollar symbol speaks for itself. The same colors, glitter for topping a candle and oils as listed for the Shango Money lightning sigil are appropriate for this one. This symbol works really well when applied to a deep green candle. Lodestone or Hematite can help attract money and work well with this seal.

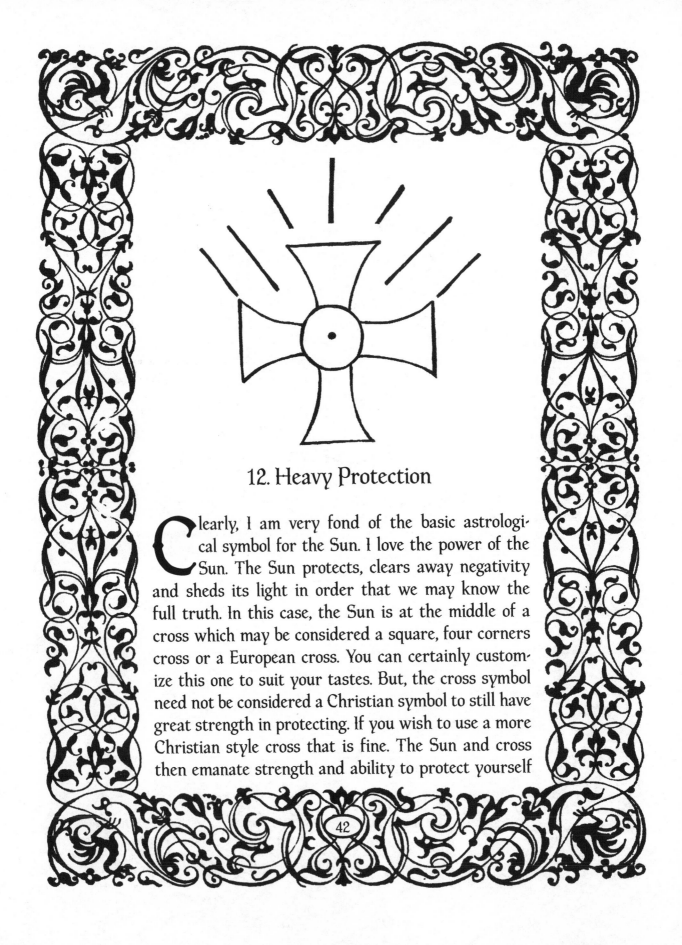

12. Heavy Protection

Clearly, I am very fond of the basic astrological symbol for the Sun. I love the power of the Sun. The Sun protects, clears away negativity and sheds its light in order that we may know the full truth. In this case, the Sun is at the middle of a cross which may be considered a square, four corners cross or a European cross. You can certainly customize this one to suit your tastes. But, the cross symbol need not be considered a Christian symbol to still have great strength in protecting. If you wish to use a more Christian style cross that is fine. The Sun and cross then emanate strength and ability to protect yourself

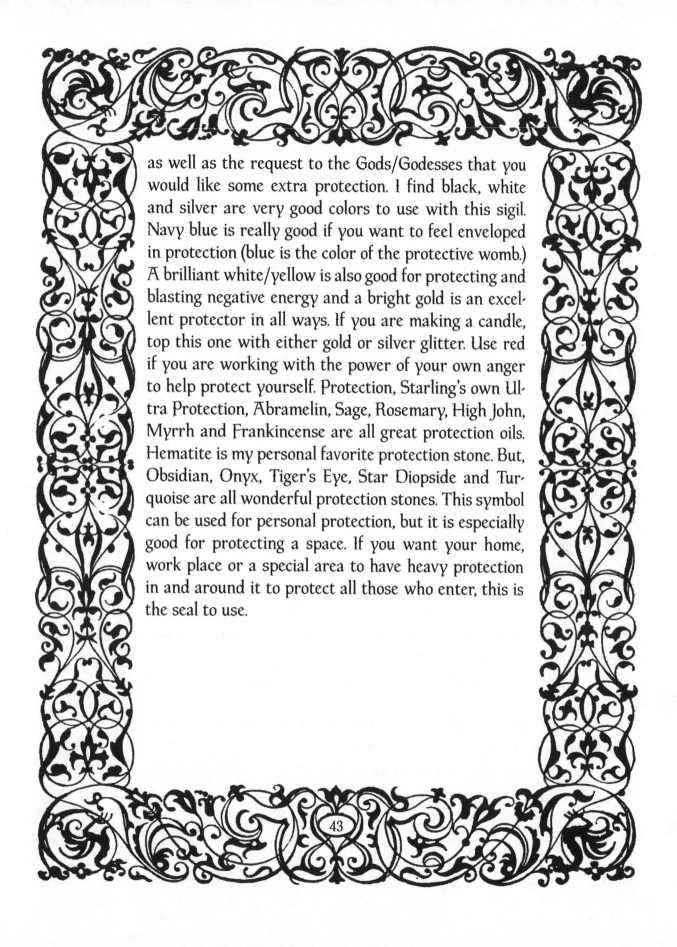

as well as the request to the Gods/Godesses that you would like some extra protection. I find black, white and silver are very good colors to use with this sigil. Navy blue is really good if you want to feel enveloped in protection (blue is the color of the protective womb.) A brilliant white/yellow is also good for protecting and blasting negative energy and a bright gold is an excellent protector in all ways. If you are making a candle, top this one with either gold or silver glitter. Use red if you are working with the power of your own anger to help protect yourself. Protection, Starling's own Ultra Protection, Abramelin, Sage, Rosemary, High John, Myrrh and Frankincense are all great protection oils. Hematite is my personal favorite protection stone. But, Obsidian, Onyx, Tiger's Eye, Star Diopside and Turquoise are all wonderful protection stones. This symbol can be used for personal protection, but it is especially good for protecting a space. If you want your home, work place or a special area to have heavy protection in and around it to protect all those who enter, this is the seal to use.

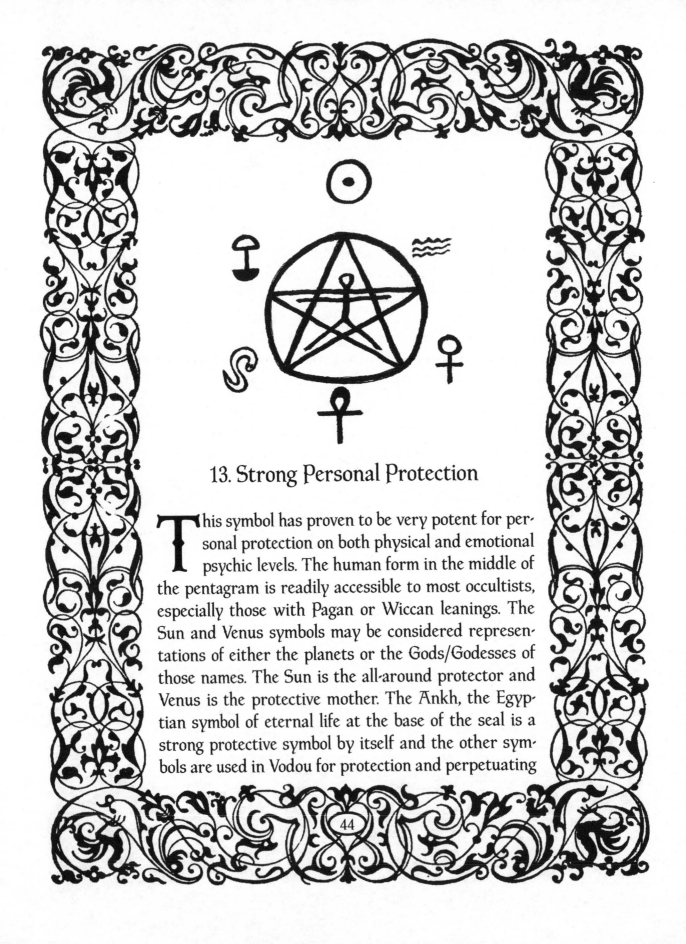

13. Strong Personal Protection

This symbol has proven to be very potent for personal protection on both physical and emotional psychic levels. The human form in the middle of the pentagram is readily accessible to most occultists, especially those with Pagan or Wiccan leanings. The Sun and Venus symbols may be considered representations of either the planets or the Gods/Godesses of those names. The Sun is the all-around protector and Venus is the protective mother. The Ankh, the Egyptian symbol of eternal life at the base of the seal is a strong protective symbol by itself and the other symbols are used in Vodou for protection and perpetuating

life. This with black, white, silver and gold is a very useful seal for protecting yourself under all sorts of circumstances. If glittering the top of a candle, use gold or silver or black glitter if you can find it. The same oils and stones listed for the Heavy Protection seal are also perfect to use with this one.

14. Protection and Peace

I designed this seal years ago when I was doing spell work to protect my mother who was in the middle of a very difficult situation. She had to travel to her home town in Rhode Island in the middle of a hurricane. My mother had survived a hurricane when she was a child and is understandably terrified of them. At the same time she was counting on the kindness of members of a part of the family she had not dealt with in decades to pick her up at the train station in the middle of this weather and not be holding years worth of pent-up anger. My mother's train got to Rhode Island safely in the middle of a full-blown hurricane and

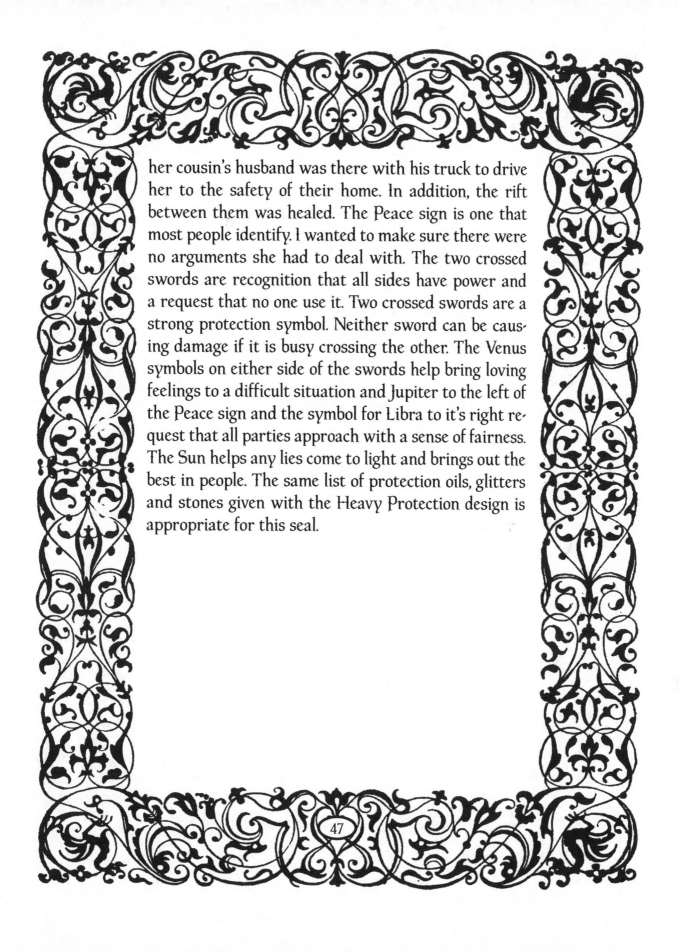

her cousin's husband was there with his truck to drive her to the safety of their home. In addition, the rift between them was healed. The Peace sign is one that most people identify. I wanted to make sure there were no arguments she had to deal with. The two crossed swords are recognition that all sides have power and a request that no one use it. Two crossed swords are a strong protection symbol. Neither sword can be causing damage if it is busy crossing the other. The Venus symbols on either side of the swords help bring loving feelings to a difficult situation and Jupiter to the left of the Peace sign and the symbol for Libra to it's right request that all parties approach with a sense of fairness. The Sun helps any lies come to light and brings out the best in people. The same list of protection oils, glitters and stones given with the Heavy Protection design is appropriate for this seal.

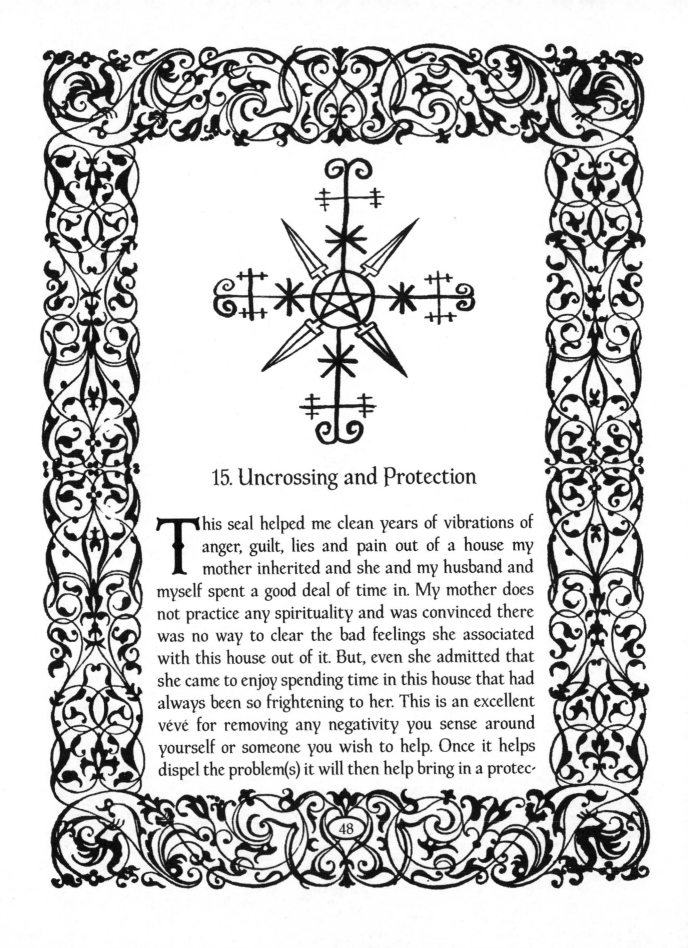

15. Uncrossing and Protection

This seal helped me clean years of vibrations of anger, guilt, lies and pain out of a house my mother inherited and she and my husband and myself spent a good deal of time in. My mother does not practice any spirituality and was convinced there was no way to clear the bad feelings she associated with this house out of it. But, even she admitted that she came to enjoy spending time in this house that had always been so frightening to her. This is an excellent vévé for removing any negativity you sense around yourself or someone you wish to help. Once it helps dispel the problem(s) it will then help bring in a protective shield in order that "crossing" doesn't just come back all over again. The design is a mixture of Vodou symbols representing the Kalfou (crossroads), Legba/Elegba (guardian of the crossroads of life, protector), European protection symbols, the swords, here in an even number covering all corners of one's life equally and the pentagram at the middle representing the soul and a strong protection symbol unto itself. Personally, I like to keep this symbol simple. I like black on white paper or silver ink/paint on black paper. If you are using the symbol on a candle the same color schemes should apply and top the candle with either gold or silver glitter. Again, the list of oils and stones for the other protection candles such as Heavy Protection work really well with this seal.

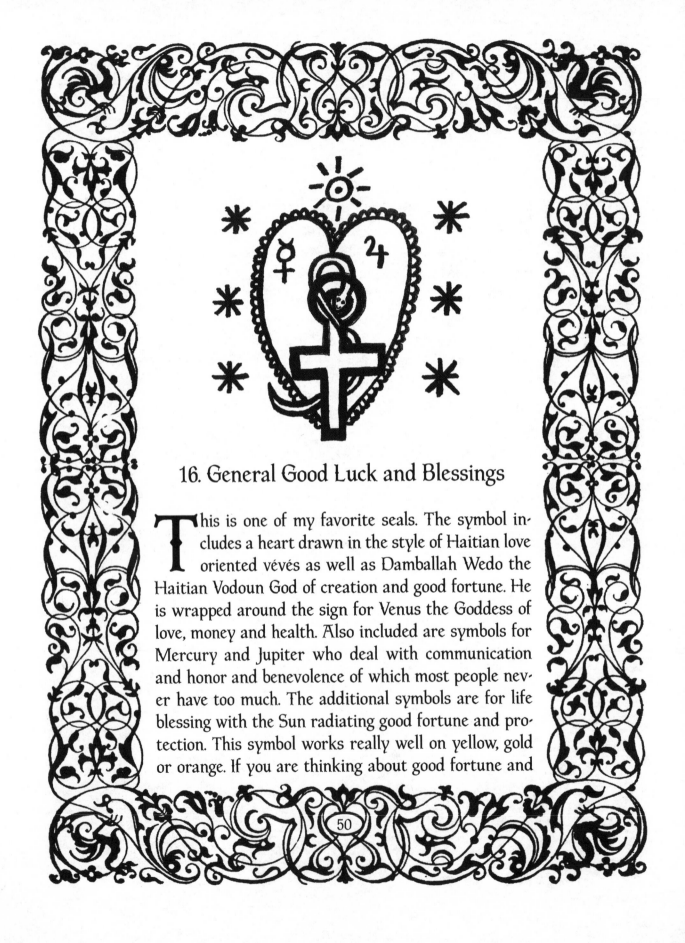

16. General Good Luck and Blessings

This is one of my favorite seals. The symbol includes a heart drawn in the style of Haitian love oriented vévés as well as Damballah Wedo the Haitian Vodoun God of creation and good fortune. He is wrapped around the sign for Venus the Goddess of love, money and health. Also included are symbols for Mercury and Jupiter who deal with communication and honor and benevolence of which most people never have too much. The additional symbols are for life blessing with the Sun radiating good fortune and protection. This symbol works really well on yellow, gold or orange. If you are thinking about good fortune and

blessings in a romantic or friendship sort of way pink is a good color. You can top a candle with this veve with almost any color glitter you like, but only use black if you are trying to give yourself or someone else some sexual good luck. Venus or Tonka Bean are my favorite oils for this sigil, however Fast Luck, Nine Fruits or something similar such as Starling's own Nine Fruits of Life, Van Van, Marie Laveau's Voodoo Luck, Lodestone, Allspice, Orange, High John or Cinnamon are all oils that would work just as well.

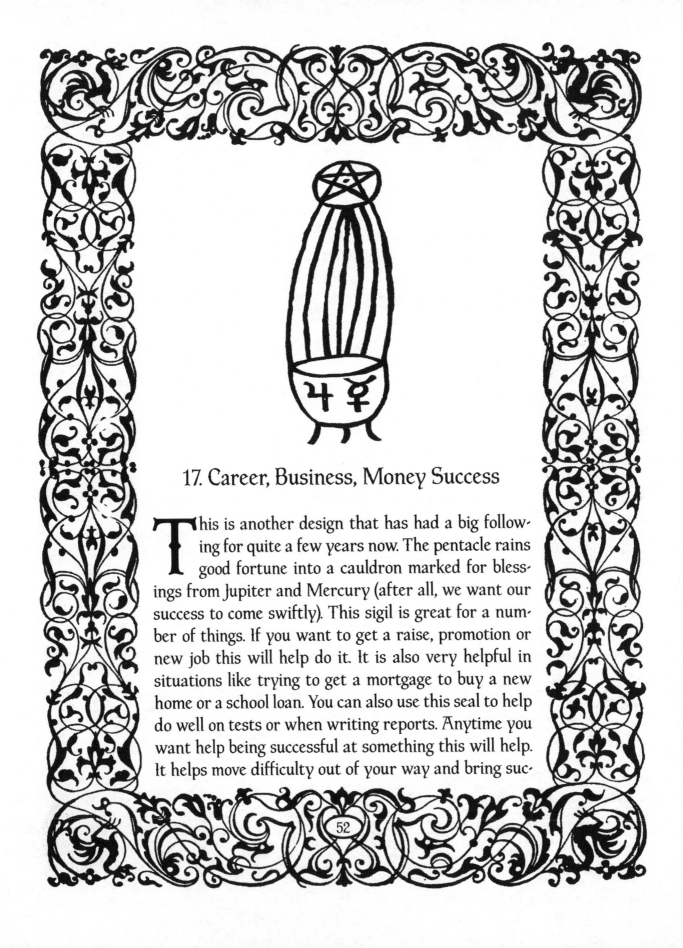

17. Career, Business, Money Success

This is another design that has had a big following for quite a few years now. The pentacle rains good fortune into a cauldron marked for blessings from Jupiter and Mercury (after all, we want our success to come swiftly). This sigil is great for a number of things. If you want to get a raise, promotion or new job this will help do it. It is also very helpful in situations like trying to get a mortgage to buy a new home or a school loan. You can also use this seal to help do well on tests or when writing reports. Anytime you want help being successful at something this will help. It helps move difficulty out of your way and bring suc-

cess at the same time. Orange or gold are great colors here. If you want to add an extra punch of energy saying to the gods, 'I deserve success at this. I've worked hard and I've had a really tough time lately,' use yellow. Glitter the top with gold or green if you're dealing with a very financially oriented issue. Success, Abramelin or Sandalwood oil are perfect for this seal.

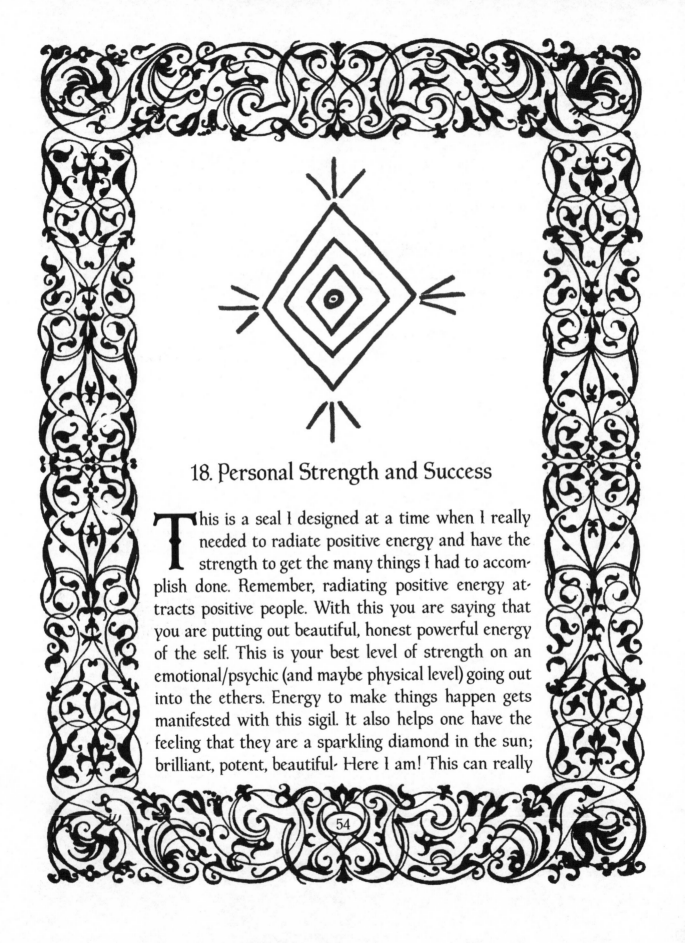

18. Personal Strength and Success

This is a seal I designed at a time when I really needed to radiate positive energy and have the strength to get the many things I had to accomplish done. Remember, radiating positive energy attracts positive people. With this you are saying that you are putting out beautiful, honest powerful energy of the self. This is your best level of strength on an emotional/psychic (and maybe physical level) going out into the ethers. Energy to make things happen gets manifested with this sigil. It also helps one have the feeling that they are a sparkling diamond in the sun; brilliant, potent, beautiful. Here I am! This can really help get even the most stubborn of projects moving. The usual color for this is purple. I love to use silver on purple for this one, especially if I am doing a candle. The best topping glitter is silver. Stones that work well with this symbol are diamond, cubic zirconia or rhinestone. Clear quartz or smoky quartz works well if it is a piece at least one inch in length. The oils you might use in conjunction with this seal are Abramelin, Starling's Clean, Clear Path, Starling's Fiery Blast of Will, Vetiver or Amber Musk.

19. Grounding for the Psyche

Some people are more prone to anxiety and feeling out of sorts than others. For anytime you are feeling that way, this is a wonderful seal to help you get your bearings back. This design has a strong effect on the psyche. The Sun nourishes and protects itself in the middle of the pyramid of mind, body and spirit. Two circular walls of protection for stability surround the triangle, blessing symbols are on either side. At our feet the pentagram star for inner wisdom and the square cross for balance at our head. The best colors for this are white, brown, green, and purple. If you want to glitter a candle top, gold is the best for grounding. The kinds of oils to use with this seal have to be oils that make you feel safer and therefore are a rather personal decision. Your zodiac birth oil or the oil for the planet that rules your sign might feel right to you. Amber, Myrrh, Nutmeg or Allspice (which also lifts the spirit) would all be good oil choices. This symbol etched or drawn on a piece of Hematite is an excellent talisman.

20. Simple Tranquility and Harmony

The astrological symbol for the moon, itself representing harmony and balance looks down over the eternal yin-yang symbol. The yin-yang is the ancient Asian symbol for balance and harmony between all the elements and the male and female energies. The stars call to mind a serene evening sky. Together, they conjure feelings of peace and comfort. Meditating with this symbol for even a few minutes a day can help even the most frenetic minds focus. Imagine yourself surrounded by a beautiful midnight blue. The colors to use with this design are deep blue, silver, black and white. This sigil on deep blue with silver,

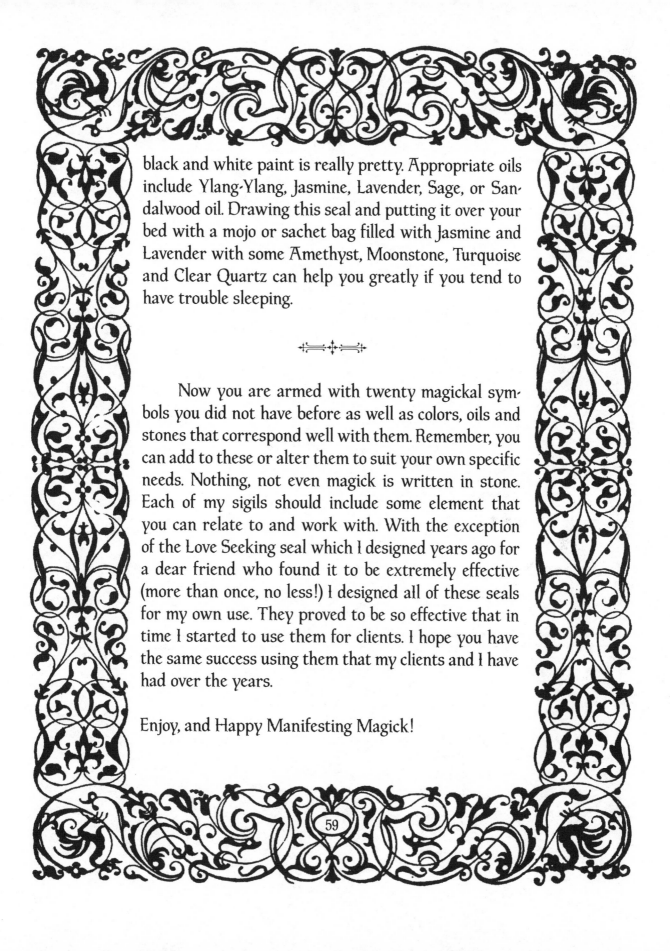

black and white paint is really pretty. Appropriate oils include Ylang-Ylang, Jasmine, Lavender, Sage, or Sandalwood oil. Drawing this seal and putting it over your bed with a mojo or sachet bag filled with Jasmine and Lavender with some Amethyst, Moonstone, Turquoise and Clear Quartz can help you greatly if you tend to have trouble sleeping.

Now you are armed with twenty magickal symbols you did not have before as well as colors, oils and stones that correspond well with them. Remember, you can add to these or alter them to suit your own specific needs. Nothing, not even magick is written in stone. Each of my sigils should include some element that you can relate to and work with. With the exception of the Love Seeking seal which I designed years ago for a dear friend who found it to be extremely effective (more than once, no less!) I designed all of these seals for my own use. They proved to be so effective that in time I started to use them for clients. I hope you have the same success using them that my clients and I have had over the years.

Enjoy, and Happy Manifesting Magick!